Mega LOL Joke Book for Kids

Hilarious Knock-Knocks, Poems, Riddles, Puns, and More Silly Fun for Ages 6 to 12

Jordan Strong

© **Copyright Jordan Strong 2025 - All rights reserved.**

The content within this book may not be reproduced, duplicated or transmitted without direct written permission from the author or the publisher.

Under no circumstances will any blame or legal responsibility be held against the publisher, or author, for any damages, reparation, or monetary loss due to the information contained within this book. Either directly or indirectly. You are responsible for your own choices, actions, and results.

Legal Notice:

This book is copyright-protected. This book is only for personal use. You cannot amend, distribute, sell, use, quote, or paraphrase any part of this book's content without the author's or publisher's consent.

Disclaimer Notice:

Please note the information contained within this document is for educational and entertainment purposes only. All effort has been expended to present accurate, up-to-date, reliable, and complete information. No warranties of any kind are declared or implied. Readers acknowledge that the author is not engaging in rendering legal, financial, medical, or professional advice. The content within this book has been derived from various sources. Please consult a licensed professional before attempting any techniques outlined in this book.

By reading this document, the reader agrees that under no circumstances is the author responsible for any losses, direct or indirect, which are incurred as a result of the use of the information contained within this document, including, but not limited to, — errors, omissions, or inaccuracies.

Contents

1. Chapter 1 — 1
   Q & A
2. Chapter 2 — 11
   Knock-Knocks
3. Chapter 3 — 19
   Riddles
4. Chapter 4 — 25
   Tongue Twisters
5. Chapter 5 — 33
   One-Liners
6. Chapter 6 — 43
   Silly Poems
7. Chapter 7 — 55
   School Jokes
8. Chapter 8 — 63
   Animal Jokes

9. Chapter 9   71
   Seasonal/Holiday

10. Chapter 10   85
    Story Jokes

11. Bonus   91
    Roses are Red

Keep the Laughs Going!   95

Also by Jordan Strong   97

Chapter 1
Q & A

Why don't robots ever get scared? They've got *nerves of steel.*

Why was the battery so bossy?
It always wanted to be *in charge*!

Why did the pencil get promoted? It had a *point*!

Why did the backpack break up with the suitcase?
It had *too much baggage.*

What do clouds wear under their pants? *Thunderwear!*

Why was the broom late? It *swept in.*

Why did the banana go to the talent show?
Because it had a-peel!

What did the sock say to the foot? "You *toe-tally* rock!"

How do you make a tissue dance? Put a little *boogie* in it.

Why did the cookie go to therapy? It felt *crumby*.

Why did the teddy bear skip dessert? Because it was *stuffed*.

What's orange and sounds like a parrot? A *carrot*.

Why did the moon skip dinner? It was *full*.

What did the tomato say to the other tomato during a race? *"Ketchup!"*

Why did the spider buy a laptop? To surf the *web*.

Why did the tomato turn red? It saw the *salad dressing*.

Why did the paper get an award? For being *write* on!

What did the clock say to the alarm? "You really *tick* me off!"

Why was the belt arrested? For *holding up pants*.

Why did the bicycle take a nap? It was *two-tired*.

Why was the fish blushing?
It saw the *ocean's bottom*.

What's the best time to go to the dentist? *Tooth-hurty.*

Why don't lentils tell secrets?
Because they always *spill the beans*.

What do elves do after school? Their gnome-work.

Why did the calendar break up with the clock?

It needed more *time* alone.

What do you call a dinosaur with an extensive vocabulary?

A *thesaurus!*

Why was the lightbulb so confident? It knew how to *shine.*

What did the fork say to the knife?

"You're looking *sharp* today!"

What's a pirate's favorite letter?

You'd think it's *R*, but it's the *C* they love!

What kind of shoes do ninjas wear? *Sneakers.*

Why don't crayons ever win races?

Because they always *draw*.

What did the microwave say to the popcorn?

"You're really *poppin'* today!"

Why can't your nose be 12 inches long?

Because then it would be *a foot*.

Why did the pirate get kicked off the trampoline?

He was too *plank-y*.

What did one volcano say to the other? "I *lava* you!"

Why did the grapes go to the party?

They heard it was *jammin'*.

What's a vampire's favorite fruit?
Neck-tarines.

Why did the apple stop in the middle of the road?

It ran out of *juice*.

What did the left shoe say to the right shoe?

"We make a great *pair!*"

Why did the scarecrow become a motivational speaker?

It was *outstanding in its field*.

Why did the pancake fail the test? It *flipped* out.

*Why do potatoes make great detectives?
They keep their eyes peeled.*

Why did the cereal bring an umbrella? In case of a *milk storm*.

Why was the sandwich nervous? It was in a *jam*.

Why was the ice cream acting weird?
It was having a *meltdown*.

What did the glue say to the paper? "I'm *stuck* on you."

Why did the balloon sit down in class?
It was ready to *pop* a quiz.

What do you call a musical insect? A *hum*-bug.

Why did the crayon break up with the pencil?
It felt *drawn away*.

Why was the broom always in trouble?
It kept *sweeping things under the rug*.

Why did the broccoli go to the gym? It wanted to be a little more stalky.

What did the cheese say when it looked in the mirror?
"*Hallou-mi!*"

What did one wall say to the other wall?
"I'll meet you at the corner!"

Why are eggs so good at telling jokes?
They always *crack you up*.

Why did the tree fail the test? It was *stumped*.

How do bees get to school? On the *buzz*.

What do pirates eat on their sandwiches? *Arrr-ugula*.

Try Not to Laugh Challenge
Silly Voices

Take turns reading jokes in the silliest voice you can (robot, whisper, opera singer, squeaky mouse).
Try not to laugh while listening!

Chapter 2
Knock-Knocks

Knock knock. Who's there?
Broccoli. Broccoli who?
Broccoli doesn't have a last name!

Knock knock. Who's there?
Howard. Howard who?
Howard you like to be knocked on all day?

Knock knock. Who's there?
Ya. Ya who?
Nope, I'd rather use Google or Edge!

Knock knock. Who's there?
Olive. Olive who?

Olive you so much it hurts!

Knock, knock. Who's there?
Lettuce. Lettuce who?
Lettuce in, it's freezing out here!

Knock, knock. Who's there?
Cow says. Cow says who?
No silly, cow says *moo*!

Knock, knock. Who's there?
Ice cream. Ice cream who?
Ice cream every time I see a spider!

Knock, knock. Who's there?
Yodel-ay-hee. Yodel-ay-hee who?
Wow, you're good at yodeling!

Knock, knock. Who's there?
Dishes. Dishes who?
Dishes the police, open up!

Knock, knock. Who's there?

Nana. Nana who?
Nana your business!

Knock, knock. Who's there?
Atch. Atch who?
Bless you!

Knock, knock. Who's there?
Peas. Peas who?
Peas be quiet, I'm hiding from my chores!

Knock, knock. Who's there?
Stopwatch. Stopwatch who?
Stopwatch you're doing and listen to me!

Knock, knock. Who's there?
Yo-yo. Yo-yo who?
Yo-yo wanna hear more jokes?

Knock, knock. Who's there?
Piano. Piano who?
Piano any good jokes?

Knock, knock. Who's there?

Bacon. Bacon who?

Bacon me crazy with all this knocking!

Knock, knock. Who's there?

Alpaca. Alpaca who?

Alpaca the suitcase, you load the car!

Knock, knock. Who's there?

Justin. Justin who?

Justin time for a snack!

Knock, knock. Who's there?

Kenya. Kenya who?

Kenya open the door already?

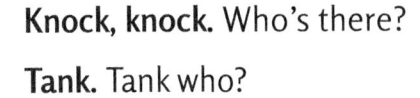

Knock, knock. Who's there?

Tank. Tank who?

You're welcome!

Knock, knock. Who's there?

Butter. Butter who?

Butter let me in before I melt!

Knock, knock. Who's there?
Scold. Scold who?
Scold outside! Let me in!

Knock, knock. Who's there?
Pecan. Pecan who?
Pecan through the window, I saw you dance!

Knock, knock. Who's there?
Waffle. Waffle who?
Waffle you do if I don't stop knocking?

Knock, knock. Who's there?
Zoom. Zoom who?
Zoom do you think you are knocking this late?

Knock, knock. Who's there?
Nacho. Nacho who?
Nacho cheese! It's mine!

Knock, knock. Who's there?
Kiwi. Kiwi who?
Kiwi be friends?

Knock, knock. Who's there?
Turnip. Turnip who?
Turnip the music, I love this song!

Knock, knock. Who's there?
Disco. Disco who?
Disco-nnected, can you hear me?

Knock, knock. Who's there?
Owl. Owl who?
Owl be seeing you later!

Knock, knock. Who's there?
Gusto. Gusto who?
Gusto go now—bye!

Knock, knock. Who's there?
Harry. Harry who?

Harry up and answer the door!

Knock, knock. Who's there?
Bean. Bean who?
Bean a while since I saw you!

Knock, knock. Who's there?
Dime. Dime who?
Dime to tell another joke?

Knock, knock. Who's there?
Cheddar. Cheddar who?
Cheddar get going before it gets cheesy!

Knock, knock. Who's there?
Cereal. Cereal who?
Cereal-ously, open the door!

Knock, knock. Who's there?
Noodle. Noodle who?
Noodle lot of silly people around here!

Knock, knock. Who's there?

Moose. Moose who?

Moose you every day!

Knock, knock. Who's there?

Icy. Icy who?

Icy you hiding behind the couch!

Knock, knock. Who's there?

Hugo. Hugo who?

Hugo first—I'm tired of knocking!

Knock, knock. Who's there?

Radio. Radio who?

Radio not, here I come!

Try Not to Laugh Challenge
Frozen Funny Face

Make the silliest face you can and freeze for 20 seconds.
Other players try to stare at you without laughing.
If they laugh, you win!

Chapter 3
Riddles

The more you take, the more you leave behind. What am I?
Footsteps.

I'm full of holes, but I can still hold water. What am I?
A sponge.

What must be broken before you can use it?
An egg.

What has a neck but no head?
A bottle.

What has a spine but no bones?   *A book.*

What has hands but can't clap?

A clock.

I fly without wings, I cry without eyes. What am I?

A cloud.

What has one eye but can't see?

A needle.

What gets wetter the more it dries?   *A towel.*

I go up but never come down. What am I?   *Your age.*

What can you catch but not throw?   *A cold.*

What goes up and down but never moves?   *A staircase.*

What has words but no grammar, pages but no chapters?

A dictionary.

What can you hold in your left hand but not in your right?

Your right hand.

What kind of cup doesn't hold water? *A hiccup.*

What begins with T, ends with T, and has T in it? *A teapot.*

What has an eye but doesn't blink? *A hurricane.*

The more you take away from me, the bigger I get. What am I?
A hole.

What has a head and a tail but no body? *A coin.*

What comes once in a minute, twice in a moment, but never in a thousand years?
The letter M.

What kind of band never plays music? *A rubber band.*

What can fill a room but takes up no space? *Light.*

What goes through cities and fields but never moves? *A road.*

What has stripes but no color, pages but no stories?

A notebook.

What is full of keys but can't open any doors? ***A piano.***

What word is spelled incorrectly in every dictionary?
Incorrectly.

What invention lets you look right through a wall? *A window.*

What is as light as a feather, but the strongest person can't hold it for long?

Their breath.

What has many teeth but can't bite? *A comb.*

What kind of room has no doors or windows? *A mushroom.*

Where does today come before yesterday? *In a dictionary.*

What has no legs but can run? *A nose or a river.*

What begins and ends with an E but only has one letter?

An envelope.

What is easy to lift but hard to throw? *A feather.*

I'm tall when I'm young and short when I'm old. What am I?

A candle.

What gets bigger the more you share it?
Happiness or a smile.

What has ears but can't hear? *A cornfield.*

What has a bottom at the top? *Your legs.*

What do you throw out when you want to use it and bring it in when you don't?

An anchor.

What comes down but never goes up? *Rain.*

What travels around the world while staying in one spot?

A postage stamp.

What's full of words but never speaks? *A book.*

What has legs but doesn't walk? *A table.*

What starts with a P, ends with an E, and has thousands of letters?

The post office.

What kind of coat is always wet when you put it on?

A coat of paint.

```
Try Not to Laugh Challenge
Banana Phone Game

Pretend a banana is a phone. Call your friend and tell them a joke without laughing. If you laugh mid-call, the banana hangs up on you.
```

Chapter 4
Tongue Twisters

Six slippery snails slid slowly seaward.

Crispy crackers crackle and crunch crisply.

Whistling winds whip white woolly weasels.

She sells seashells by the seashore.
The shells she sells are surely seashells.
So if she sells shells on the seashore,
I'm sure she sells seashore shells.

Fuzzy ferrets flung funny feathers from France.

Fresh fried fish served fast on Fridays.

Silly Sammy swiftly shouts seven silly songs.

Tiny turtles tiptoe through the tulip trail.

Red rodents resting on rainy rocks.

Bobby baked big blueberry banana bread.

Five friendly frogs flipping flat flapjacks.

Two tiny tigers tiptoed toward a tall tree.

Purple penguins paddle past plump puffins.

If a dog chews shoes, whose shoes does he choose?

Peter Piper picked a peck of pickled peppers.
A peck of pickled peppers Peter Piper picked.
If Peter Piper picked a peck of pickled peppers,
Where's the peck of pickled peppers Peter Piper picked?

Zany zebras zoomed zigzagging through the zoo.

Sassy Sally swiftly sews seven socks.

Jumpy jackals juggle jellybeans joyfully.

Larry's lizard likes licking lemon lollipops.

Cheeky chickens chuckle while chasing chocolate cheese chips.

Violet vikings vacuum vanilla velvet vests violently.

Bouncing bananas battle buttery balloon beasts.

Freddy's froggy flip-flops flopped four feet forward.

Chubby cheeked chipmunks chomping cheesy crackers.

Wacky wizards whistled while whipping whipped cream.

Fred's friend Fran flips flapjacks faster than Fred.

Grumpy ghosts gulp gooey gummy grapes groggily.

Milo's miniature monkeys made messy macaroni mountains.

Pam's panda plays ping-pong with pineapples politely.

Sticky snails slide slowly singing slippery silly songs.

Greedy goats gobble green grapes grossly

Ten timid turtles trying to talk tough.

Wendy's windy window whistles wildly.

Betty bought a bit of butter, but the butter was bitter, so Betty bought a better bit of butter to make the bitter butter better.

Cute kangaroos carry cookies in checkered cases.

Unique New York, unique New York. You know you need unique New York.

Shy sheep should sleep in a shed.

Tommy the talkative turtle told ten tall tales today.

Zany zebras zip through zesty zucchini zones.

Giggling geese gobbled green gummy grapes.

Twirly turtles tango in top hats on Tuesday.

Brave blue birds bounce between bamboo branches.

A skunk sat on a stump. The skunk thought the stump stunk, and the stump thought the skunk stunk.

**Try Not to Laugh Challenge
Slo Mo**

Say a tongue twister in super slow motion. Laughing at your own slowness? That counts as a loss!

Chapter 5
One-Liners

I used to be afraid of hurdles, but **I got over it.**

I drew a picture of a sandwich. **Now I'm hungry and confused.**

I put my phone in airplane mode. **It flew off the table.**

I tried to eat a clock. **It was time-consuming.**

I once had a pet rock. **It didn't roll with me.**

I tried to write a joke about pizza, but **it was too cheesy.**

I have a joke about a broken pencil. **Never mind—it has no point.**

I made a belt out of watches. **It was a waist of time.**

I named my cat "Wi-Fi." **Now it finally connects with me.**

I opened a bakery for dogs. Business is ruff.

I put a bandage on my laptop. **It had a byte.**

I made friends with a tornado. **He really blew me away.**

I tried to organize a hide and seek contest. **But good players are hard to find.**

I'm afraid for the calendar. **Its days are numbered.**

I only know 25 letters of the alphabet. **I don't know Y.**

I took my pet rock for a walk. It was a drag.

I met a vampire at the dentist. **He was fang-tastic.**

I used to hate facial hair. **But then it grew on me.**

I told my dad to stop acting like a flamingo. **He had to put his foot down.**

I stayed up all night wondering where the sun went...**then it dawned on me.**

I used to be a banker—but **I lost interest.**

I named my dog "Five Miles" so I can say **I walk Five Miles every day.**

I got hit with a soda can yesterday. **Luckily, it was a soft drink.**

I opened a bakery with no dough—**it was a crumby idea.**

The frog parked illegally—he got toad.

The pirate didn't shower before walking the plank—**he just washed up on shore.**

I told my friend 10 jokes to make him laugh—**but no pun in ten did**.

One day, I asked my dog, "What's two minus two?" **He said nothing**.

I got locked in a bakery overnight—**it was a sweet situation**.

I once told a joke about vegetables. It was **corny**.

I'm reading a book about glue. I just can't seem to put it down.

I couldn't write a joke about herbs—**I just didn't have the thyme**.

The calendar factory fired me—**I took a few days off**.

I tripped over my Wi-Fi—**I guess it was a hotspot**.

I bought a boat because **I was feeling a bit adrift**.

I named my horse Mayo—**and sometimes Mayo neighs**.

The snowman wanted a job—he heard the work was chill.

The best way to watch a fly fishing tournament is via **live stream**.

I'm friends with all electricians — **we have good current connections.**

I'm not lazy. **I'm on energy-saving mode.**

The duck bought lipstick—she put it on her bill.

The bakery caught fire—**the bread was toast.**

I made a pencil with two erasers. **It was pointless.**

I asked the library for a book on disappearing. **They said it was gone.**

I don't trust stairs. **They're always up to something.**

I told a joke about construction. **I'm still working on it**.

I tried to catch fog. **I mist**.

I told my dog a joke. He pawsed to think about it.

I used to be a baker. **But I couldn't make enough dough.**

I watched a movie about elevators. **It had its ups and downs**.

I tried to tell a joke about paper. **It was tearable**.

I made a joke about a pencil sharpener. **It didn't make the cut**.

I bought a snow globe. It gave me a little shake-up.

I wrote a song about tortillas. **Actually, it's more of a wrap.**

I asked the librarian if books about paranoia were available — **she whispered, "They're right behind you."**

The football team's bakery burned down—**now they have turnovers.**

I couldn't figure out how to put on my seatbelt—**then it clicked.**

**Try Not to Laugh Challenge
Water Cheeks**

Each person takes a sip of water and holds it in their cheeks.
Another person tells 3 jokes or riddles.
If anyone spits out the water, they lose!

Chapter 6
Silly Poems

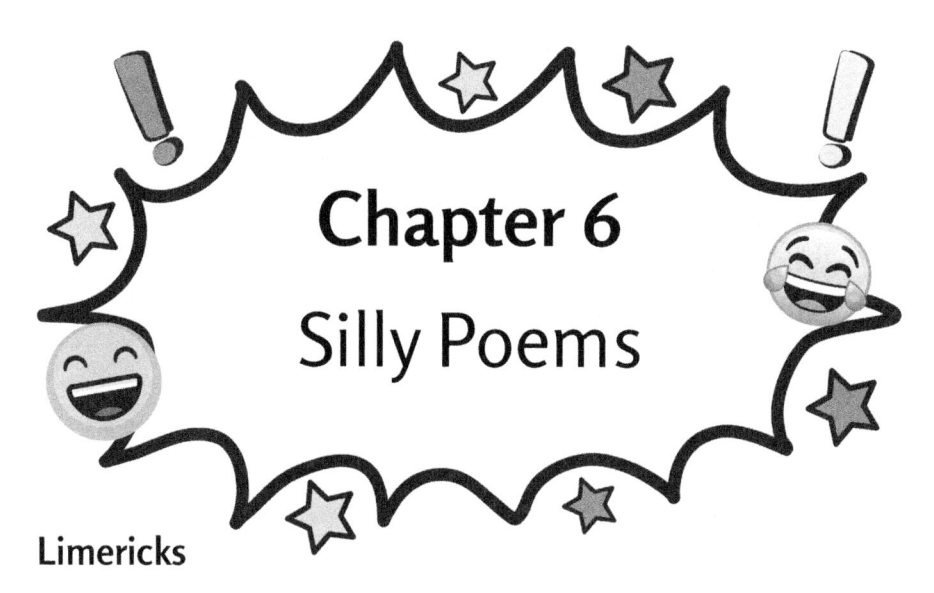

Limericks

A limerick is a short, funny poem with five lines and a specific rhythm and rhyme. Lines 1, 2 and 5 rhyme. Lines 3 and 4 rhyme. It has a humorous twist or punchline at the end.

A turtle who wanted to fly,

Made wings out of pizza and pie.

He flapped with a shout,

And just spun about—

But at least he gave it a try!

A monkey who juggled three cakes,

Did flips over rivers and lakes.

But one little slip,

Made frosting all drip—

And now he just juggles pancakes.

A bear with a bubblegum hat,
Got stuck on a trampoline mat.
He bounced once or twice,
Which felt rather nice—
Then landed right next to a cat!

A pirate who sailed on the sea,
Got tangled up chasing his tea.
His parrot would shout,
"Just figure it out!"
While sipping some cocoa with glee.

There once was a cat from Peru,
Who painted her whiskers bright blue.
She strutted with pride,
While others just sighed—
"She's starting a trend, it's true!"

A fish who wore goggles to school,
Thought looking cool was the rule.
He bumped into glass,
Then laughed with his class—
"I guess that's what happens to cool!"

There once was a frog in a tree,
Who thought he was buzzing a bee.
He croaked out a song,
But it came out all wrong,
And now he just ribbits off-key!

A snail with a racing obsession,
Had dreams of speedy progression.
He zoomed with such flair,
Though still going "there"—
Took three months to reach a concession!

There once was a pig who could rhyme,

But always a little off-time.

He snorted out tunes,

In awkward balloons—

But claimed it was "poetry prime!"

A chicken who wanted to skate,

Laced up and rolled through the gate.

She twirled with such flair,

And flew through the air—

But landed in someone's lunch plate!

A duck with a bowtie so red,

Wore pancakes upon his head.

When someone said "Why?"

He gave a quick sigh—

"They're tastier up there," he said.

A kangaroo hopping on sand,

Played banjo with only one hand.

He sang with a grin,

A song full of spin—

Now he's got his own rock band!

There once was a goat in a dress,

Who made quite a fashion-y mess.

She tripped on her hem,

Then winked and said, "Ahem!

I'm fabulous nonetheless!"

A dog who could rollerblade fast,

Zipped by and just giggled right past.

He barked with delight,

At squirrels in flight—

Then slid into lunch at last!

A llama who danced in the rain,

Slipped and then spun down the lane.

He grinned ear to ear,

And shouted, "I'm clear!

But now I have mud on my mane!"

A cow with a ukulele,

Would play it each single day-ly.

She mooed out a song,

While chewing along—

And called it her moosical medley.

A zebra who loved to eat pie,

Tried throwing one up to the sky.

It fell with a splat,

Right onto a cat—

Who meowed, "Next time aim more high!"

A snake who liked jumping on beds,

Kept bumping his scaly green heads.

He tried to explain,

"It's fun though insane!"

Then coiled up and juggled some breads.

A squirrel who liked doing ballet,

Would twirl in the treetops all day.

She leapt with a cheer,

While chipmunks said, "Dear,

You're nutty in every good way!"

> **Try Not to Laugh Challenge**
> **Foot Tickle**
>
> Have someone tickle your foot lightly while you read the joke.
> If you laugh, you're officially a featherweight.

Clerihews

A clerihew is a very short and silly poem about a person. It has 4 lines: Line 1 rhymes with line 2, and line 3 rhymes with line 4.

Albert Einstein

Thought time was just fine.

But he got quite stressed,

When he forgot how to get dressed!

Harry Potter

Dropped his magical blotter.

He tried to take notes,

But they all turned into goats.

Amelia Earhart

Knew flying was an art.

She soared through the air,

Till her plane lost a wheel somewhere.

Mozart the Great

Played music quite late.

He banged on the keys,

While sneezing from cheese.

Cleopatra

Told jokes ever after.

Her eyeliner game?

Was better than fame.

Neil Armstrong

Sang a moon-landing song.

But forgot the words,

And was chased by moon-birds.

Sherlock Holmes

Lost his combs.

He said with a grin,

"I'll deduce where they've been!"

Dr. Seuss

Turned moose into juice.

He rhymed without care,

Wearing green underwear.

Marie Curie

Mixed potions in a hurry.

Her glow-in-the-dark stew,

Lit up the whole zoo.

Jane Austen

Burnt her toast in Boston.

She sipped her tea,

And wrote books about me.

Queen Elizabeth

Ruled with royal breath.

She sneezed with a "HACHOO!"

And knighted her shoe.

Napoleon Bonaparte

Had a tiny shopping cart.

He bought shortbread and jam,

And yelled, "I am who I am!"

Batman

Used a frying pan.

Not to cook or to bake,

But to battle a cake.

Leonardo da Vinci

Painted a squirrel named Pinchy.

It posed with flair,

While brushing its hair.

Santa Claus

Once got stuck in the gauze.

He slipped on a toy,

Left by a clumsy elf boy.

William Shakespeare

Had a very long ear.

He overheard cheese,

And wrote sonnets with ease.

Thor the god

Found thunderstorms odd.

He said, "Where's the fun,

Without a bit of sun?"

Elsa from Frozen

Kept the fridge wide open.

She shouted with glee,

"More ice for my tea!"

Albert the Alligator

Became an elevator.

He opened his jaws,

And said, "Please mind the claws."

**Try Not to Laugh Challenge
One Word at a Time Joke**

In pairs, try to make up a joke by saying one word each back and forth.
You can't laugh while building it!

Chapter 7
School Jokes

Why did the music teacher go to jail? For getting in *treble*.

Why did the kid bring a flashlight to school?
In case he had a *bright idea!*

Why did the math book look so sad?
Because it had *too many problems!*

What did the pencil say to the paper?
"You've got a good point!"

What did the science book say to the history book?
"You're so *old school.*"

What's a snake's favorite class?
Hiss-tory.

Why was the teacher wearing sunglasses in class?

Because *her students were so bright!*

Who is the king of the classroom?   *The ruler!*

Why did the student eat his homework?

Because the teacher said *it was a piece of cake!*

Why don't science teachers trust atoms?

Because they make up everything!

Why was the music room so cold?

Because it had too many fans!

What's a pirate's favorite subject?
Arrrrrrt!

What's the best way to talk to a school of fish?

Drop them a line!

Why did the clock get detention?   It kept *tocking back!*

Why did the student bring a ladder to school?

Because he was going to *high school!*

What kind of school do you go to if you're a surfer?

Boarding school!

What did the teacher do with the student's report on cheese?

She *grated* it!

Why did the student take a ruler to bed?

To see how *long* he could sleep!

What's a math teacher's favorite place to shop? *Times Square!*

What do you call a math teacher who's always cold?

A *numb*-er cruncher!

Why did the teacher write on the window? Because she wanted her lesson to be clear!

Why was the locker acting so shy?

It didn't want to *open up!*

Why was the history book always worried?

It had too many *dates!*

Why did the kid bring a pillow to class? For *nap time*-tables!

What do you get when you cross a teacher with a vampire? Lots of blood tests!

Why did the science project get detention?

It *exploded* in class!

What do you call a class full of ducks? A *quackademic!*

Why did the art class turn into a zoo?

Too many *wild* brush strokes!

What did the crayon say to the pencil sharpener?

"Stop *grinding* my gears!"

Why did the bell get promoted?

It always knew when to *ring in* a good idea!

Why did the glue get a time-out?

It *stuck* its nose in everyone's business!

Why did the student do math in the cafeteria?

Because she heard there would be *pi!*

Why did the chalkboard break up with the eraser?

It was tired of being *wiped out!*

What's the smartest insect at school?   The *spelling bee!*

Why did the student sit on his homework?

He wanted to *do it on the fly.*

Why did the elephant bring a suitcase to school? It was ready to pack in more knowledge.

Why was the computer cold in class? It left its *Windows* open!

What did the paper say to the glue? "I'm *sticking* with you!"

Why was the eraser always so chill?

It could handle all kinds of *mistakes*.

What did the notebook say during roll call?

"Present—and accounted four pages!"

Why don't you ever fight with an English teacher?

They always have the *last word.*

Why was the gym teacher always so positive?
She knew how to *work things out!*

What did the janitor say when he jumped out of the closet?
"Supplies!"

What's a witches favorite subject?   *Spell-ing!*

**Try Not to Laugh Challenge
Reverse Joke Telling**

Say the punchline first, then try to explain the setup.

"Because it was stuffed!... Why did the turkey not eat dessert?"

Try not to laugh at how backward it gets!

Chapter 8
Animal Jokes

What do you call a pig who tells jokes? A *comediham*.

What do you call a dinosaur who sleeps all the time?
A dino-*snore*.

Why don't cats play poker in the jungle? Too many *cheetahs!*

What do you call a cat that can sing? *Meow-donna!*

Why did the squirrel bring a notebook?
It wanted to take *nuts!*

How does a dog stop a video?
It presses the *paws* button.

What did the peanut say to the elephant? "You *crack* me up!"

What do you call a dog magician? A *labracadabrador!*

What kind of stories do ducks like? *Feather* tales.

Why don't ants ever get sick? They have tiny *ant-bodies.*

What's a cat's favorite TV show? *Paw* & Order.

Why did the parrot sit on the computer?

To *tweet* from a better perch!

What do bees use to brush their hair?

A *honeycomb!*

What do you get when you cross a shark and a snowman?

Frostbite.

Why was the cheetah always late?

It kept stopping for *fast food!*

What's a cat's favorite color?   *Purr-ple.*

Why don't leopards play hide-and-seek?

Because they're always *spotted.*

Why do owls never get in trouble?   They're *too wise.*

Why did the snail paint an 'S' on its car?

So people would say, "Look at that *S-car-go!*"

Why did the frog call the plumber?   It had a *leap* in the sink.

How does a penguin build its house?   *Igloos* it together.

What did the snail say when it got a ride on the turtle's back?

Wheeeee!

What do you call an alligator in a vest?   An *investigator!*

Why did the horse go behind the tree?   To change his *jockeys!*

What do you get when you cross a fish and an elephant?
Swimming trunks!

What kind of key opens a banana?   A *monkey*!

What do you call a lazy kangaroo?   A *pouch potato.*

What's a frog's favorite candy? *Lollihops.*

How do you catch a squirrel?
Climb a tree and *act like a nut*!

Why don't seagulls fly over the bay?
Because then they'd be *bagels.*

Why did the duck get detention?
It couldn't stop *quacking* jokes!

What do you call a bear with no teeth?

A *gummy* bear!

Why did the pig become an actor?
Because he was a real *ham!*

Why did the chicken join the band?
Because it had *drumsticks!*

What do cows read with breakfast?
The moos-paper!

What do you get when you cross a sheep and a kangaroo?
A *woolly jumper!*

What do you call a rabbit who tells jokes?
A *funny bunny!*

What do you call a snake who works for the government?
A civil *serpent!*

What do you call a dog that can tell time?
A *watch dog!*

What do frogs wear on their feet?

Open *toad* sandals!

Why did the owl get promoted?

Because he was a *wise* guy!

What do you call a dog who designs buildings?

A *bark-itect!*

Why did the turtle cross the road?

To get to the shell station!

Why did the giraffe get bad grades?

Because he had his *head in the clouds!*

Why did the crab never share?

Because he was *shellfish!*

Why do fish live in saltwater?

Because *pepper* makes them sneeze!

Why did the lion eat the tightrope walker?

He wanted a *well-balanced* meal!

What's a shark's favorite sandwich?

Peanut butter and jellyfish!

Why don't owls use cell phones?

Because they don't give a *hoot* about texting!

What do you call a group of musical whales?
An orca-stra!

Why did the cat join the Red Cross?

Because it wanted to be a *first aid kit-ty!*

Why did the pig bring sunscreen to the beach?

It didn't want to turn into *bacon!*

What did the duck say after making a joke?

"I'm *quackin'* myself up!"

What's a cow's favorite game?

Moo-no!

> **Try Not to Laugh Challenge**
> **Animal Sounds**
>
> Read a short story—but replace random words with animal sounds (moo, quack, meow).
> Listeners try not to laugh!

Chapter 9
Seasonal/Holiday

Spring and Easter

Why are bees always buzzing in spring?
Because they don't know the words!

What do you call a grumpy bunny?
A *hop-timist* in training!

Why did the tree start taking dance lessons?
It wanted to *shake off* the leaves from last year!

What do you get when you cross a rabbit with a shellfish?
An *oyster* bunny!

How does the Easter Bunny stay in shape? *Eggs*-ercise!

How does the Easter Bunny keep his fur looking nice?

Hare spray!

Why was the Easter Bunny so grumpy?

He was having a bad *hare* day!

What do you call a line of Easter bunnies jumping backward?

A *receding hare-line!*

Why did the Easter Bunny cross the road?

Because the chicken had the day off!

What happened to the Easter egg that misbehaved?

It got *egg-spelled!*

What kind of stories does the Easter Bunny like best?

Ones with *hoppy* endings!

Why shouldn't you tell an Easter egg a joke?

Because it might *crack* up!

What kind of music does the Easter Bunny like?

Hip-hop!

Summer and Independence Day

What did the sand say to the tide?

"Long time no sea!"

What did one flag say to the other flag?

Nothing—it just waved!

Why did the duck say "bang"?

Because he was a fire-quacker!

How do you make a hot dog stand on the 4th of July?

Take away its chair!

Why did the watermelon start a band?

It had the melon-choly blues!

Why don't bananas ever get sunburned?

Because they always *peel!*

Why did the firecracker go to school?

To become a little *brighter!*

What's the best way to catch a summer tan?

Use a net made of sunshine!

What do you call an American drawing?

A Yankee doodle!

What do you call a snowman on the 4th of July?

A puddle with spirit!

What kind of tea did the American colonists want?

Liber-tea!

What's red, white, blue, and green?

A seasick Uncle Sam!

Why don't you knock on America's door on July 4th?

Because freedom *rings!*

Halloween

Knock, knock. Who's there?
Goblin. Goblin who?
Goblin up all the Halloween candy!

Why did the ghost go to art school?
To learn *boo-shading.*

What's a ghost's favorite dessert? *I-scream!*

Why didn't the skeleton go to the party?
Because he had no *body* to go with!

Why don't skeletons take tests?
They don't have the *guts.*

Why did the ghost bring a pencil to class?

In case it had to *draw a blank*.

What do you call a witch's garage?
A broom closet!

What kind of music do mummies like best?
Wrap music!

Why did the vampire get a job at the blood bank?
He always wanted to work with his favorite drink!

Why don't zombies eat clowns?
Because they taste *funny!*

What's a ghost's favorite ride at the amusement park?
The roller-*ghoster!*

How do you fix a broken jack-o'-lantern?
With a pumpkin *patch!*

What is a skeleton's favorite instrument?
The *trom-bone!*

What did one bat say to the other?

Let's *hang* out later!

What do you call a cleaning skeleton?

The "grim *sweeper*"!

What kind of makeup do ghosts wear?

Mas-*scare*-a!

Why do vampires always seem sick?

Because they're always *coffin*!

Why did the witch go to school?

To improve her *spell*-ing!

What's a monster's favorite side dish?

Mashed *BOO-tatoes!*

Why was the mummy late for school?

He got *wrapped up* in something!

What do you call a werewolf who uses bad manners?

A howler!

What kind of pants do ghosts wear?

BOO-jeans!

Why didn't the skeleton cross the road?

Because he didn't have the *guts!*

What does a ghost put on his toast?

BOO-berry jam!

Thanksgiving

What do you get when you cross a turkey with a centipede?

Drumsticks for everyone!

What did the mashed potatoes say to the gravy?

"Cover me—I'm going in!"

Why did the turkey bring a microphone to dinner?

Because it was ready to *roast!*

Why did the turkey get kicked out of school?

Because it used *fowl* language!

What did the turkey say to the computer?

Google, google, google.

Why did the cranberries turn red?

Because they saw the turkey *dressing!*

What sound does a limping turkey make?

Wobble wobble!

What do you call a running turkey?

Fast food!

Why did the turkey sit at the drum set?

Because it already had the *drumsticks!*

What's the best dance to do on Thanksgiving?

The *turkey* trot!

Why don't turkeys eat dessert?

Because they're already *stuffed!*

Winter and Christmas

What do you get when you cross a snowman and a dog?

Frostbite!

Why did the mitten get invited to the party?

Because it was a *perfect fit!*

How does a snowman get around?

By riding an *"icicle!"*

What's a snowman's favorite snack?

Ice Krispies Treats!

Why don't mountains get cold in the winter?

Because they wear *snowcaps!*

What do you call a snowman with a six-pack?

An *abdominal* snowman!

Why did Rudolph get a bad report card?

Because he *went down in history!*

Why was the Christmas tree so bad at knitting?

Because it kept dropping its *needles!*

What do reindeer hang on their Christmas trees?
Horn-aments!

Why was the elf so good at music?

Because he had great *'elf'* control!

What's Santa's favorite kind of music?

Wrap music!

Why did the ornament go to school?

To get a little *"tree"* education!

What do you call a cat on the beach during Christmas?
Sandy Claws!

What did Mrs. Claus say to Santa when he looked outside?
"Looks like rain, dear."

Why did the gingerbread man go to school?
To become a *smart cookie!*

Why don't you ever see Santa in the hospital?
Because he has *private "elf"* care!

What do you get if you cross a bell with a skunk?
Jingle smells!

What's a sheep's favorite Christmas song?
"Fleece Navidad!"

How does Santa keep his suit wrinkle-free?
He uses *Claus*-tarch!

What do elves use to take notes in school?

Their *elf*-abet!

Why was the snowman looking through the carrots?

He was *picking his nose!*

**Try Not to Laugh Challenge
Frozen Audience**

One person is the **comedian** and tells jokes, makes silly faces, or says goofy things.

Everyone else must stay **frozen** like statues—no laughing, smiling, or moving!

If someone laughs or moves, they're out. Last statue standing wins!

Chapter 10
Story Jokes

The Talking Dog

A boy finds a sign that says, "Talking Dog for Sale."

He runs inside and asks, "Can I meet the dog?"

The owner nods, and the dog says, "Hi there. I used to work for the police. Then I did movies. Now I'm retired."

"The boy yells, "WOW! Why are you selling him?"

The owner says, "Because he **lies all the time!**"

The Dog Who Did Homework

Max told the teacher, "My dog did my homework."

The teacher raised her eyebrows.

"He barked the answers," Max insisted.

"And what grade did he get?" she asked.

Max grinned. "An A... for arf-fort!"

The Kid and the Genie

A kid finds a magical lamp. He rubs the lamp, and a genie appears.

He says to the kid, "What is your first wish?"

The kid says, "I wish I were rich!"

The genie replies, "It is done! What is your second wish, Rich?"

Two Kids Camping

Two kids are camping in their backyard. It was late at night and they wanted to know the time.

They start singing at the top of their lungs.

Then one of their neighbors threw open his window and yelled,

"Cut the noise! Don't you know it's 3 o'clock in the morning?"

The Man and the Librarian

A man walks into a library, approaches the librarian and says, "I'll have a cheeseburger and fries, please."

The librarian says, "Sir, you know you're in a library, right?"

"Sorry," he whispers. "I'll have a cheeseburger and fries, please."

The Bear and the Waiter

A bear walks into a restaurant and says, "I want a grilled ... cheese."

The waiter says, "Why the big pause?"

The bear replies, "I don't know. I was born with them."

The Kangaroo and the Rabbit

"Oh, no!" the kangaroo groaned to her friend, the rabbit. "The forecast calls for rain."

"What's the problem with that?" asked the rabbit. "We could use some rain."

"Sure," the kangaroo said. "But that means my kids will have to play inside all day!"

The Dog that Plays Chess

A man went to visit a friend and was amazed to find him playing chess with his dog.

The man watched the game in astonishment for a while.

"I can hardly believe my eyes!" he said. "That's the smartest dog I've ever seen."

"He's not so smart," the friend replied. "I've beaten him three games out of five."

The Businessman and the Handyman

A businessman went into the office and found an inexperienced handyman painting the walls.

The handyman was wearing two heavy parkas on a hot summer day.

Thinking this was a little strange, the businessman asked the handyman why he was wearing the parkas on such a hot day.

The handyman showed him the instructions on the can of paint.

They read: "For best results, put on two coats."

**Try Not to Laugh Challenge
Joke Charades**

Act out the punchline of a joke without saying anything.

Others guess the joke—but they can't laugh while watching!

Try miming "a chicken crossing the road!"

Bonus
Roses are Red

Roses are red
Violets are blue
My sandwich just vanished—
I think that it flew!

Roses are red
Violets are blue
I tried to eat soup
With just one shoe.

Roses are red
Violets are blue
I named my left sock
Sir Dances-A-Lot Too.

Roses are red
Violets are blue
I told a bad joke
Now the chairs booed me too.

Roses are red
Violets are blue
My cat stole my blanket
And claims it as new.

Roses are red
Violets are blue
I stuck all my homework
To the dog with some glue.

Roses are red
Violets are blue
I tried to bake brownies—
Now the oven is glue.

Roses are red

Violets are blue

If pizza is missing

It probably was you.

Roses are red

Violets are blue

My robot just sneezed

And said, "Achoo-boo!"

Roses are red

Violets are blue

This poem makes no sense,

But neither do you!

Try Not to Laugh Challenge
Clap & Gasp

After every joke or poem, instead of laughing, everyone must **clap three times and say "Oh wow!"** with a straight face.
If you forget or laugh, you're out!

Keep the Laughs Going!

We hope you had a laugh!

If this book brought giggles to your home or classroom, we'd love it if you could take a moment to leave a quick review on Amazon.

Your feedback helps other folks discover the fun and keeps us inspired to create even more silly jokes for kids like yours!

Simply scan the QR code below to leave a review

Thank you for helping spread the laughs!

Also by Jordan Strong

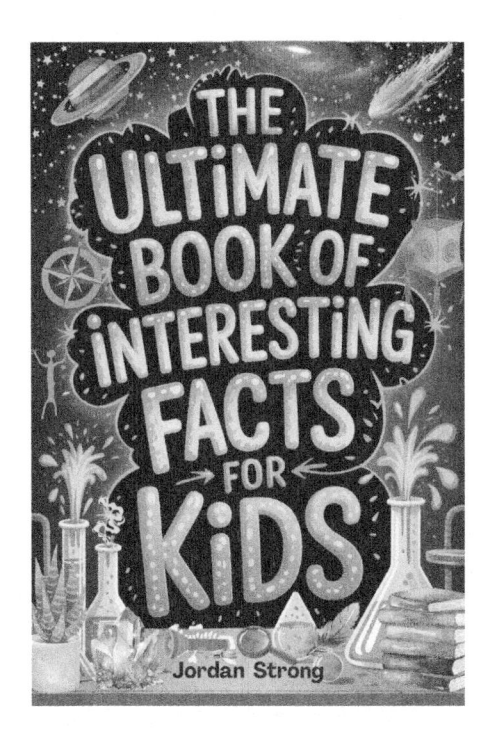

Printed in Dunstable, United Kingdom

67356771R00057